SOUTH HOLLAND PUBLIC LIBRARY

3 1350 00184 8011

W9-BLS-820

South Holland Public Library
South Holland, Illinois

DISCARD

AMISTAD

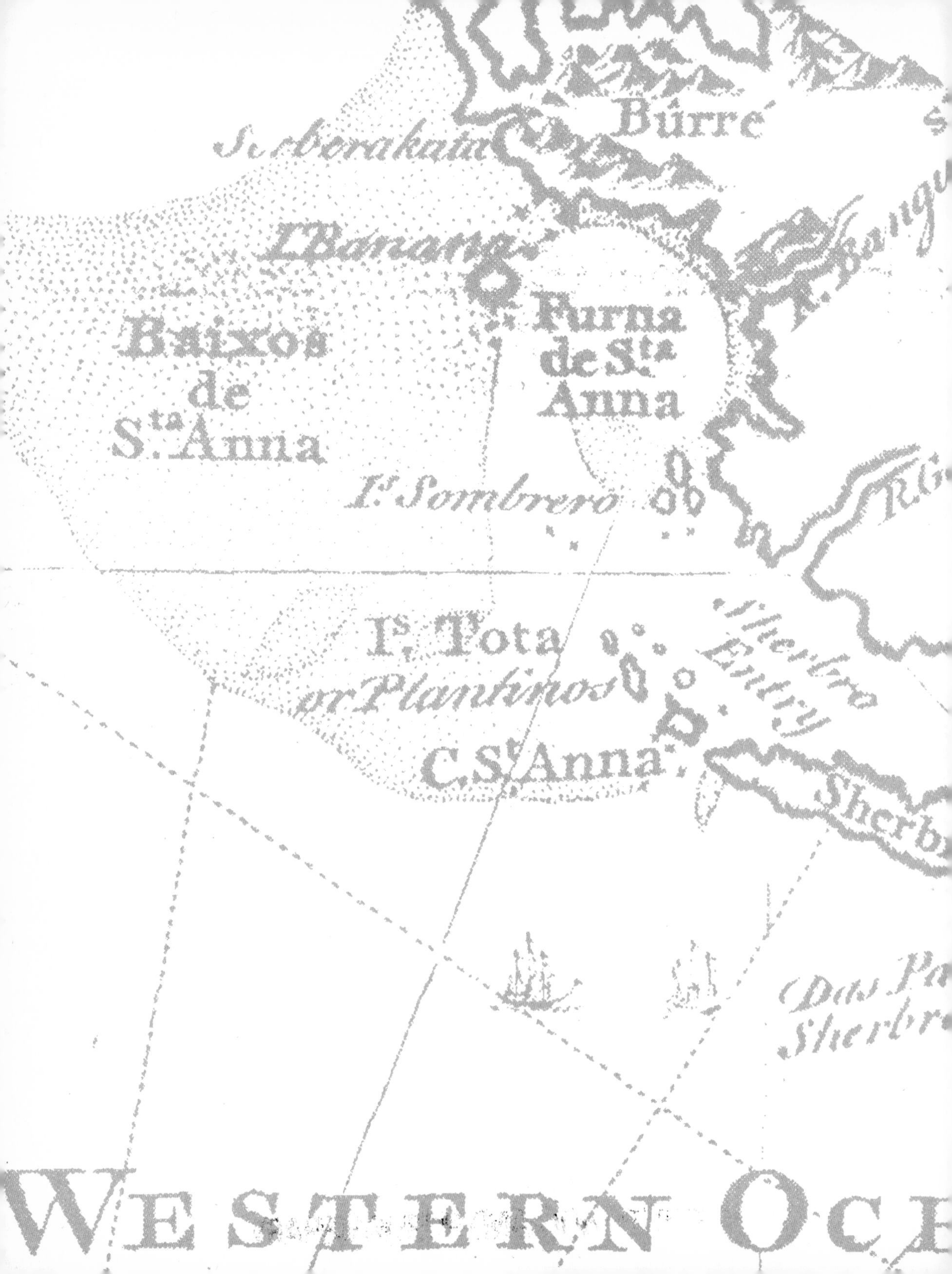

Burré

Seberakata

I. Banana

Furna
de Sta
Anna

Baixos
de
Sta Anna

I. Sombrero

Is. Tota
or Plantinos

Silentro
Entry

C. St Anna

Sherb

Das Pa
Sherbr

WESTERN OCE

AMISTAD

A Long Road to Freedom

Walter Dean Myers

DUTTON CHILDREN'S BOOKS / NEW YORK

DISCARD
SOUTH HOLLAND PUBLIC LIBRARY

3 1350 00184 8011

The endpapers are authentic courtroom sketches of some of the
illegally enslaved captives. Sources of photographs and prints are
cited on page 95.

Text copyright ©1998 by Walter Dean Myers
TM & ©1997 DreamWorks

All rights reserved. No part of this publication may be reproduced or
transmitted in any form or by any means, electronic or mechanical,
including photocopy, recording, or any information storage and
retrieval system now known or to be invented, without permission in
writing from the publisher, except by a reviewer who wishes to quote
brief passages in connection with a review written for inclusion in a
magazine, newspaper, or broadcast.

CIP Data is available.

Published in the United States by Dutton Children's Books,
a member of Penguin Putnam Inc.
375 Hudson Street, New York, New York 10014

Designed by Judith Henry

Printed in USA   First Edition
10 9 8 7 6 5 4 3 2 1   ISBN 0-525-45970-7

The African Chief

Chained in the market-place he stood,
A man of giant frame
Amid the gathering multitude
That shrunk to hear his name—
All stern of look and strong of limb,
His dark eyes on the ground;
And silently they gazed on him
As on a lion bound.

Vainly, but well, that chief had fought;
He was a captive now,
Yet pride, that fortune humbles not,
Was written on his brow.
The scars his dark, broad bosom wore
Showed warrior true and brave;
A prince among his tribe before,
He could not be a slave.

—WILLIAM CULLEN BRYANT

Acknowledgments

Special thanks to the Farmington Historical Society and especially to Marguerite W. Yung, who were very helpful in the research in that area.

Mark Shenise at the Methodist Archives at Drew University was more than helpful and exceedingly patient in helping me to track down material pertaining to the Mendi Mission in Sierra Leone.

Special thanks also to my lovely wife, Constance.

Two Notes About the African Names

The names of the Africans are, in all cases, spelled the way they sound to an English-speaking person. Sometimes it is possible only to approximate the sounds. I've seen the names spelled different ways even in the same newspaper article. Foone, Funi, Funni? Which do you use? Authorities in Sierra Leone have given the pronunciation of Sengbe's name their blessing, but even he adopted the use of an English form (Joseph Cinque) for convenience. To complicate matters, there was no known written form of Mande when Sengbe was in the United States.

It was interesting to me, though, that of all the Africans, the only one whose name Ruiz wrote on the *traspaso* that approximated an African name was that of Sengbe. Clearly, Sengbe was a force even before the *Amistad* captives took over the ship.

CONTENTS

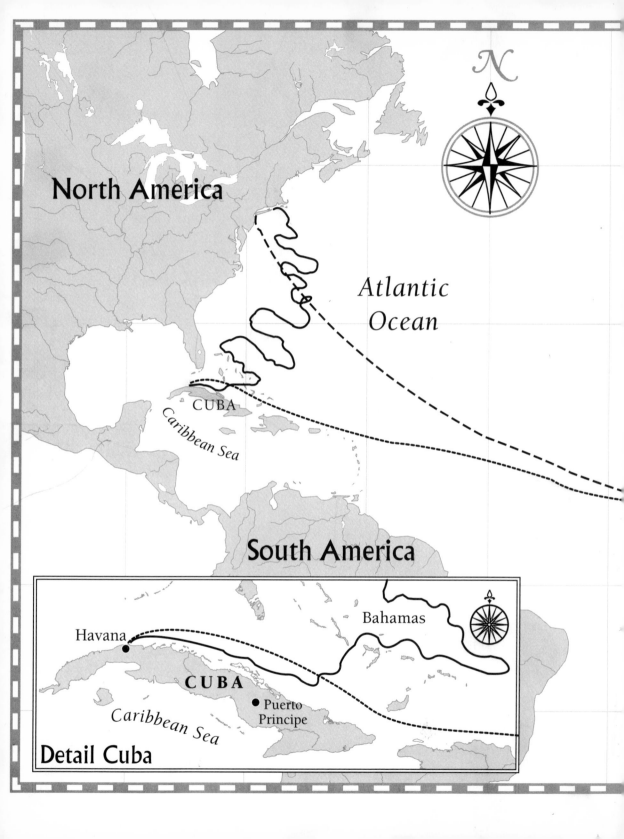

North America

Atlantic
Ocean

CUBA

Caribbean Sea

South America

Bahamas

Havana

CUBA

Puerto
Principe

Caribbean Sea

Detail Cuba

The Voyages of the *Amistad* Captives

- - - - - - - - - - Voyage of *Tecora* to Cuba
——————— Voyage of *Amistad* to United States
– – – – – – – – – Voyage of *Gentleman* to Africa

Africa

SIERRA
LEONE
MENDELAND
Lomboko
Harbor

Detail United States

New Haven ●   New London ●

Culloden Point

New York
City ●   Long Island

*Montauk
Point*

Map by Claudia Carlson

TIME LINE

JANUARY 1839	Sengbe captured in West Africa
APRIL 1839	*Tecora* takes Sengbe and others from Africa.
JUNE 1839	*Tecora* arrives in Havana.
JUNE 28, 1839	Captives put aboard the *Amistad*
JULY 1839	Captives take over the *Amistad*.
AUGUST 26, 1839	Lt. Gedney, aboard the *Washington*, captures the *Amistad*.
AUGUST 29, 1839	Preliminary hearing by Judge Judson aboard the *Washington*
SEPTEMBER 19, 1839	The defense asked for the release of the three African girls (habeas corpus), which was denied. It was ruled by Judge Thompson that the United States had no right to try the captives for murder or piracy.
SEPTEMBER 23, 1839	In district court, Judge Judson starts inquiry as to where the *Amistad* was captured.
OCTOBER 17, 1839	Ruiz and Montes arrested in New York City

NOVEMBER 19, 1839   District court hearing in Hartford, Connecticut

JANUARY 7, 1840   District court continues in New Haven, and Sengbe testifies. Judson rules on January 13 that captives are free and that Gedney, Ruiz, and Montes are entitled to salvage.

JANUARY 1840   U.S. District Attorney appeals decision to circuit court.

MAY 1840   Judge Thompson confirms district court decision. The case is then appealed to the Supreme Court.

FEBRUARY 22, 1841   Arguments begin before Supreme Court.

MARCH 9, 1841   Supreme Court affirms that *Amistad* captives are free.

MARCH 19, 1841   Captives move to Farmington, Connecticut.

NOVEMBER 27, 1841   Captives sail for Sierra Leone, West Africa.

JANUARY 1842   Captives reach Sierra Leone. It is three years since Sengbe was first captured.

AMISTAD

Prologue

AUGUST
1839

Culloden Point lies at the eastern end of Long Island, New York. It had long been a favorite place of fishermen angling for the deep-sea fish that traveled up the eastern coast of the United States. In late summer the early morning fog could completely cover the sound; but as the sun burned off the fog, strollers along the beach could see all the way across the sound to Connecticut. It was late August in 1839, and these early morning walkers were treated to a strange sight. A low black schooner was anchored off the coast. Some of her sails were badly torn; others flapped loosely in the light breeze. To experienced sailors, the rigging of the ship was odd. She looked more like a ghost ship than a working boat.

There had been reports of a possible pirate ship in the area.

One thing was soon clear to the small crowd of men gathered on the beach: The crew of the schooner was all black. An old sailor said he had seen some blacks on the shore the day before. They spoke a strange language, he said. And there was a wild look about them, something between desperation and rage.

There would be more to learn—much more. But it would take years of controversy and legal arguments that involved two American presidents and three countries before all the pieces of the mystery would be sorted out.

One of the men on the shore who had spent years sailing the seas produced a telescope and took a closer look at the schooner. There wasn't much else to see except for the name of the ship. It was called the *Amistad*.

CHAPTER 1

The Background

The year was 1839. Martin Van Buren was the eighth president of the United States. The country was at peace and prospering, but there were issues that threatened the young nation. A major issue was that of slavery.

The "peculiar institution" of slavery had existed in the North American colonies since 1619. For years, men, women, and children were taken from Africa in chains, put into sailing ships, and brought across the ocean. Many were put to work on plantations in both North and South America and on the islands of the Caribbean. Others were household domestics, miners, or lumberjacks. By 1776 the number of Africans brought across the ocean was in the millions.

When the colonies of North America banded together in 1776 to declare their independence, the question of slavery was in the minds of the founding fathers. The colonists talked about the rights of all human beings and of their own desire to be free of oppression from

Great Britain. But slavery already existed in the country that was to be. How could a nation fight a war of independence, proclaiming the freedom of all men, when many of the men within its borders were not free but slaves? These stirring words from the Declaration of Independence do not speak of slaves or slavery:

We hold these truths to be self-evident, that all men are created equal, that they are endowed by their Creator with certain un-alienable Rights, that among these are Life, Liberty, and the pursuit of Happiness.

The problem was that although the United States of America wanted freedom from Great Britain, many of the most important men

Charles-Town, May 15, 1769.
TO BE SOLD,
On Wednesday the Twenty-fourth Instant,
A choice CARGO of about 800
Prime NEGROES,
Just arrived in the Ship Jenny, Captain
RICHARD WEBSTER, directly from the
RICE or GRAIN COAST.
JOHN EDWARDS, & Co.

Africans with rice-growing experience were highly valued.

leading the fight for freedom held black people on their plantations as slaves. The slaves were considered to be the "property" of their owners.

The United States, declaring itself an independent country instead of a colony of Great Britain, went to war. At the end of this war, the Revolutionary War, the victorious Americans created a constitution. The Constitution would be the basis of all American law. It carefully laid out the rights of the American people. Many of the founding fathers wanted to end the practice of holding human beings in a state of slavery. Others wanted to continue the practice. The two sides reached an uneasy compromise: Individual states would decide if they would allow slavery or not. However, antislavery forces were able to get a clause into the Constitution that said that Congress could stop the importation of slaves in 1808. Article I, Section 9, reads:

The migration or importation of such persons as any of the States now existing shall think proper to admit, shall not be prohibited by the Congress prior to the year one thousand eight hundred and eight.

In 1807 Congress passed a law making it illegal to bring in new people to be slaves:

Be it enacted, That from and after the first day of January, one thousand eight hundred and eight, it shall not be lawful to import or bring into the United States or the territories thereof from any foreign kingdom, place, or country, any Negro, mulatto, or person of color, as a slave, or to be held to service or labor.

While it was illegal to import slaves into the United States in 1808 and thereafter, it was still legal in many states to have slaves.

Great Britain, which had once been one of the most active nations in the slave trade, outlawed slavery in England in 1787. Later, in an effort to end the slave trade throughout the world, the British made a number of treaties with other countries that were involved with the trade. One of these treaties was with Spain. In 1817 the Spanish government agreed not to take any more people from Africa and to make it illegal for its citizens to obtain any people brought from Africa for the purpose of slavery. This did not, however, free any of the slaves who were in Spain or its colonies before the ban.

So in 1839 it was illegal to bring anyone born in Africa into either the United States or Cuba as slaves. Anyone brought from Africa into the United States as a slave was to be sent back to Africa by the President. Anyone brought from Africa into Cuba was eventually to be freed and allowed to return to Africa.

Despite the ban, the need for workers in North and South America continued, and soon there were people willing to break the laws of their nations to profit from the capture and sale of humans. There were other people who believed that slavery should be immediately abolished, who were just as determined to fight against the inhuman trade. Many of these people were involved on both sides of the issues in the case of the *Amistad*.

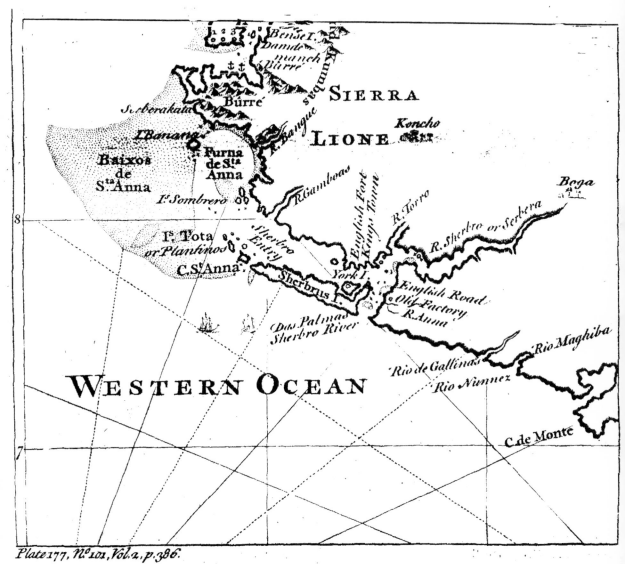

Map showing the Gallinas River (Rio de Gallinas) in Africa

The Slave Traders

Pedro Blanco had been operating on the west coast of Africa, in the area called the Grain Coast, for decades. His base of operation was near the border of Sierra Leone in the region of the Gallinas River, now called the Moa River. He built a prison at Lomboko for those unfortunate men, women, and children brought to him. The prisons were called barracoons. They are described by a fellow slave dealer, Theodore Canot, with whom Blanco did business:

> The barracoons were made of rough poles of the hardest trees, four or six inches in diameter, driven five feet in the ground and clamped together by double rows of iron bars. Their roofs were constructed of similar wood, strongly secured, and overlaid with a thick thatch of long and wiry grass, rendering the interior dry and cool.

Blanco made it clear that he would buy any healthy African brought to him. Virtually all of the Africans brought to the coastal region in which Blanco made his headquarters were brought to him by other Africans. At Lomboko the captured Africans would be put into the barracoons and held until such time as they could be transferred to a slave ship.

The Gallinas River was especially useful for Don Pedro Blanco's business. It was shallow—too shallow for a British cruiser looking for slavers but not too shallow for the canoes that carried the cap-

Barracoons owned by Pedro Blanco

tured Africans from Blanco's barracoon to the waiting ships. Everyone knew that taking people from Africa was illegal, so it had to be done under the cover of darkness or at other times when it was certain that there were no antislaving ships nearby.

An important element in the trade was the cost of the ship. The records show that a ship designed to carry from three hundred to four hundred slaves could be built for $3,750. This would be about $45,000 in today's dollars. The profit from each African captive who made it across the Atlantic Ocean in good condition was between $180 and $600, depending on where they were sold and whether the captive was a child or an adult. There would be less profit in Cuba or South America and more—a great deal more—profit in the United States. A ship that delivered 300 captives could easily have a profit of half a million dollars in today's currency.

The ships would often be abandoned after four or five trips. The reason for this clearly shows the inhumanity of the slave trade. Once taken aboard the ships, the captives would be chained belowdecks and would not be allowed to wash or to use any sort of bathroom facilities. When they had to relieve themselves, they had to do it while chained in the cramped quarters. The wooden decks they lay on were soon reeking with waste material, and the captives had to lie in it. If any of them became ill, and many did, they would still have to lie in the filth, often for weeks at a time. Eventually the wood in the decks and body of the ship would be so soaked with the waste material that no crew could stand to be on it. Then the boat would simply be abandoned and another one bought or built.

The Abolitionists

Throughout the world there have always been people who have felt strongly that to deny freedom to anyone is morally wrong and that slavery everywhere should be ended at once. In the 1800s, many of these people, called abolitionists because they wanted simply to abolish slavery, were willing to make major sacrifices to end the practice. Although they were often from religious groups such as the Quakers, they were just as often men and women who based their beliefs on what they saw as simple humanity. Lewis Tappan, Austin F. Williams, James W. C. Pennington, Robert Purvis, and John Pitkin Norton are among the abolitionists discussed in this book.

Black abolitionist Robert Purvis

The Mende captives visited the church of Rev. James W. C. Pennington in Hartford.

Other people involved were within the legal system of the United States, especially judges and lawyers, men for whom the drama of the law takes on the excitement of mortal combat. Roger Baldwin, Seth P. Staples, Theodore Sedgwick, Judge Andrew T. Judson, Judge Smith Thompson, and former president John Quincy Adams were precisely such men.

Mendeland, West Africa

JANUARY

1839

The village of Mani lay deep in the heart of that area of West Africa known to some as Mendeland. Locations in Mendeland had a number of different names, depending on who was speaking. Europeans who settled in Africa did so near the coastal areas and gave the cities and regions either European names or their own versions of the African names. A great deal of Mendeland was in the European settlement of Sierra Leone.

During the slave trade to the United States, a special premium was paid for those Africans brought from this region because of their knowledge of rice growing. Many Africans from Mendeland ended up growing rice in South Carolina. Sengbe Pieh was born and lived in Mani and earned his living as a rice farmer.

Sengbe's mother was dead, but his father lived with him and his family, which, in 1839, consisted of Sengbe, his wife, and their three children. In the history he later gave to James Covey, a translator, Sengbe said that his son's name was Gewaw. This was the family he left when he awoke one morning to travel to his fields.

Rice growing sometimes requires a number of farmers to work the fields. This is when the land is flooded with the water in which rice grows and during the harvesting season. At other times, on a small farm, a single person can tend the fields, pulling weeds and making sure that the water level is correct. When Sengbe went to his field, it was shortly after the planting season and he was alone.

The houses in Mani were built in a circle. From the edges of the village, the neighboring area could be seen for miles around. The earth was rockier there than it was in the valley, but the town was safer. Sengbe had heard of wars in Dahomey, nearly a month's distance to the southeast, but the Mende of Sierra Leone were not at war. Still, under the robe he wore draped over his shoulder was a belt to which he attached a machete.

The distance from Mani to Sengbe's fields was a short one, and Sengbe reached the fields before the sun was high. Suddenly he stopped. There were strangers on the road before him. He counted: There were four of them, and they quickly surrounded him. One of the men carried a rifle. There was a brief struggle as Sengbe fought the men, but he was soon overpowered. It was clear from the start that they didn't want to kill him. Instead they carefully placed a loop around his right wrist and tied it tightly to his neck. With his right arm in this awkward, painful position, he was helpless.

The men, who were Vai, spoke a Mande language. It was a language close enough to the one spoken by Sengbe that he could try to talk with them. It was useless. In Mendeland the Europeans had been using the Vai people for years to do their slave catching.

Sengbe was taken from place to place. He was a commodity, a

captive that could be sold. But for Africans, the selling process itself was full of danger. Many Africans involved in the slave trade were themselves seized and sold by the people who hired them. Whoever approached a European to sell an African was always in danger of being seized himself. It was a full month—a month of being held captive in small villages and trying to bargain for his release—before Sengbe was sold to a slaver and sent on the path to Lomboko.

Lomboko was an island at the mouth of the Gallinas River. Once there, Sengbe was put into a barracoon. In a few days he was taken out of the barracoon and dragged before a white man. The man was Pedro Blanco, the slave dealer.

Sengbe was young, in his mid-twenties, and quite healthy. For Pedro Blanco it was an easy purchase. What he paid for Sengbe was probably less than he paid for the bottles of Spanish brandy he was fond of serving to guests.

It was at Lomboko that Sengbe met Grabeau, another Mende man. Like Sengbe, Grabeau was a rice farmer. Together they waited two months in the prison at Lomboko to learn their fate. During that time, they talked and became friends. They were both married, but Grabeau had no children. He was shorter than Sengbe and strongly built. Sengbe thought that if they ever

Grabeau had also been a rice farmer in Sierra Leone.

Captives were taken to the slave ships in canoes like this.

had a chance to fight for their freedom, Grabeau would be a good man to have by his side. As they ate their daily ration of boiled fish and rice, they talked of regaining their freedom.

As the days passed, more and more captives were brought to Lomboko. There were men, women, and children. All were healthy; all had come from Sierra Leone. They thought that things could not get worse. They were chained up, far away from their families and villages. But they were wrong; things could get worse for the despairing Africans.

The slave trade was illegal in most parts of the world, and British ships patrolled the coastline to make sure that slaves were not being smuggled out. A treaty signed in 1836 allowed the British to destroy ships that they caught engaged in the trade. Slave dealers like Blanco knew that the fewer trips they had to make, the better. Blanco had to have the barracoons filled and then smuggle out and load onto the

ships as many of the captives as possible before his operation was spotted. It was three full months before the barracoon that Sengbe was in had enough captives to make the run through the shallow waters around Lomboko to the waiting ship.

Pedro Blanco, along with the other owners of the ship that would carry the captives across the ocean, made a final inspection of the Africans. He made them jump to see if their legs were strong. He examined their teeth and their eyes to make sure he wouldn't lose money on a sick or lame captive. Then, one night, the owners began loading them into canoes.

The Kru people lived along the coastline of Sierra Leone. They fished along the shore and out in the ocean. They were also excellent boatmen. It was in a Kru canoe that Sengbe found himself when he was taken out to a slave ship.

The *Tecora* was a large ship fitted out to accommodate the slave trade. The deck had a grating, which would allow both seawater and rain into the hold. This would have ruined regular cargo, but the opening allowed the African captives to breathe while below-decks. The ship was quickly loaded just before daybreak. The ship's captain would want to be away from the shore before sunup—and away from the possibility of being spotted by a British antislavery cruiser.

Sengbe was pushed aboard the *Tecora* and forced to go below-decks, where the Spanish crew quickly put him in chains. The height of the hold in which the captives were kept was a little over three feet.

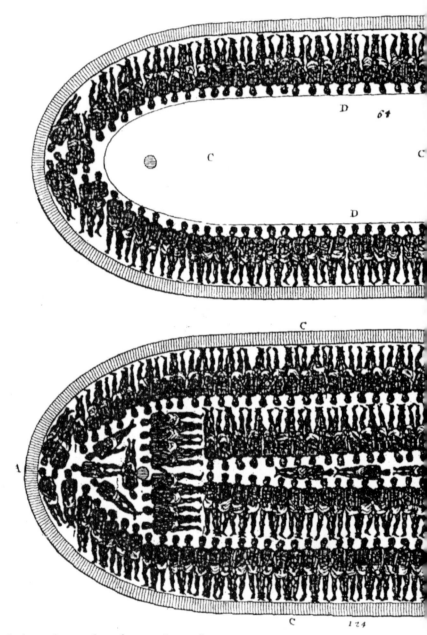

A drawing of an actual slave ship with its human "cargo"

Fig. 5

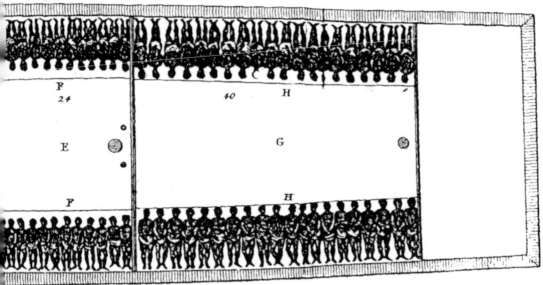

Fig. 4

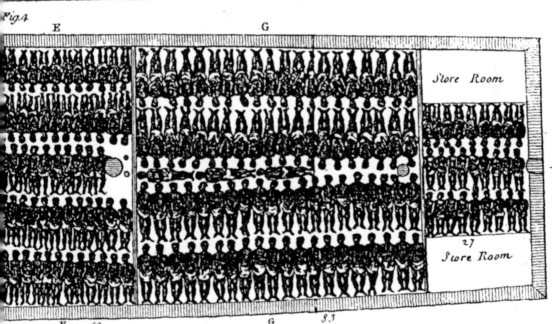

The captives had to bend over to get to their assigned places. They were packed closely together so that no one could turn without touching the person next to him.

The loading took hours, but by the time the first rays of sunshine cracked the gray morning sky, the task had been completed. The ship was already on its way.

Ships involved with the slave trade made three trips. The first part or passage would be from either Europe or the Americas to Africa. The ships would be nearly empty, carrying just enough cargo to barter for the Africans unlucky enough to be caught by the slavers. The second part of the ships' journey would be from Africa to the Americas. This was the dreaded Middle Passage, during which the human cargo would undergo nearly unbearable suffering. The third part of the journey would be the ships' return to their home ports.

Beneath the main deck, where the captives sat hour after dreary hour, the air was foul and hot. There was nowhere for them to go to relieve themselves, and the stench of human waste added to their misery. Once a day the captives were made to climb out of the hold and onto the deck. In the open air they were given a small portion of water and a meal, usually of rice or some other grain. Then they were forced to jump up and down or run in small circles on the deck. This was to keep their limbs fairly strong. Every captive who died was money lost for the slavers.

Sengbe sucked in the air as he stumbled onto the deck. The bright sun made him squint as he turned in a full circle. As far as he could see in every direction, there was nothing but water. The food was tasteless; the water was not enough to quench the thirst that had tormented him through the night. He checked the position of the sun. They were still traveling west.

The journey on the *Tecora* from Sierra Leone to Havana, Cuba, finally came to an end in June 1839. The ship put into harbor at night, and Sengbe was taken off the ship in darkness—the same way he had been put on. With the men in chains and the women and children tied together with ropes, the slavers took the captives through the streets of Havana to a barracoon. Here they were fed and given water.

Days later they were roused and lined up to be inspected yet again. The inspections were deeply humiliating as men felt the limbs of the Africans and even looked into their pants. Again they had to open their mouths so that their teeth could be examined, and they had to jump about. Any African who did not obey was instantly hit with a whip. One man in particular looked closely at Sengbe. His name, Sengbe would later learn, was Jose Ruiz. He was twenty-four years old, two years younger than Sengbe. Ruiz went to the owners of the *Tecora* and made a deal for Sengbe and forty-eight other Africans.

On Wednesday, June 28, 1839, Ruiz and his companions led the chained Africans, including Sengbe, to the riverside in Havana's harbor and loaded them onto the schooner *Amistad*.

The *Amistad* was a schooner, a relatively fast vessel that had been built in a shipyard in Baltimore, Maryland. Its name, *Amistad*, means "friendship." Onboard was the captain and owner, Ramon Ferrer. The crew consisted of Ferrer's two black slaves, Antonio and Celestino, and two white seamen. Besides the humans, the ship also carried a cargo that consisted of dishes, cloth, jewelry, and other goods. Pedro Montes, fifty-eight, a Spanish citizen living in Cuba, had bought four children—three girls and a boy. He and the children were aboard as well.

Again the captives were placed belowdecks. The schooner set out from Havana and headed, Ruiz and Montes would later state, for Puerto Principe, in the southern part of the island.

Sengbe had already been a captive for six months by the time he was pushed aboard the *Amistad*. He had tasted the cruelty of being enslaved and the inhuman ways in which the Africans were treated. He had seen the Africans beaten, seen them nearly starved to death, and seen many die on the long journey across the Atlantic Ocean. Now he watched as the crew of the *Amistad* pushed the men and children belowdecks for yet another hellish journey.

The *Amistad*, like the *Tecora*, was outfitted to carry slaves. For the owners, the schooner promised speed. For the Africans in its hold, it represented just another nightmare in what seemed to be an endless string of nightmares.

The hold of the *Amistad* was too low for any of the captives to stand. They had to crouch and then sit, one tight behind the other, their legs, wrists, and necks shackled at night. The shackles cut cruelly into their wrists and made their hands swell. During the day they were allowed to have some freedom, but never were all the irons removed at once. Several of the men were whipped.

The stench of the air belowdecks made even the simple act of breathing difficult. Some of the Africans locked in with Sengbe could not speak Mande. He spoke to the others, saying that they had to look for a way to escape. Death could be no worse than what they were going through.

Sengbe counted the seven men who held them aboard the *Amistad*. Two of them, Pedro Montes and the ship's captain, were fairly old. Sengbe realized there were enough Africans to take over the ship if they had the chance. The crew had guns—which they would use, he knew—but the Africans were from a culture that prided itself on physical fitness. And if the chance came, it would be their freedom they would be fighting for.

There were wooden crates in the hold with the Africans. One time the captives saw one of the sailors take a machete, a broad-bladed knife, from an open crate. If the captives ever got loose, they would have weapons.

The crew of the *Amistad* was sure that the Africans would not get loose. No one had ever broken the chains before. Also, the captives

The captives were bound in heavy chains.

were kept in a weakened condition as a result of dehydration. Each day they were given only one cup of water. When one man tried to quench his thirst by taking more, Ruiz ordered that he be whipped.

The captives watched and waited. They told Sengbe what they noticed. By day the whites took turns guiding the ship and guarding the Africans. Each day the captain sent either Celestino or Antonio into the hold to release the Africans in small groups to exercise on the deck, all under the watchful eyes of the armed white men.

By night all of the captives were chained belowdecks. Burna, who had been a blacksmith in Mendeland, could see how the shackles were made. There was a spring mechanism in the shackle that was opened with a tool placed in the end of the locked iron, hooked over a metal lip, then pulled. They searched the hold for a tool, any tool that they could use to open the chains. A spike was found, which they hid.

Celestino was brown-skinned and, to Sengbe, seemed without intelligence. The ship's captain would yell at him and hit him, and he, in turn, would do the same to the locked-up Africans. One day he pointed to the large pots in which he cooked the little food they ate. He took his knife and ran it mockingly under his chin, pointed again to the pots, then rubbed his fat belly. He was telling them they would be eaten!

A summer storm pushed them toward the Bahamas Channel. The trip that should have taken two days was in its third night of rough seas. To Sengbe and the other Africans, the gusts of wind and the warm rain coming through the grating that led to the deck were a welcome relief.

A furnace in Sierra Leone like the one Burna used

The men listened. They heard the gentle groaning of the ship as the wood resisted the rolling sea and the sound of water lapping against the side of the *Amistad*. From the deck above, there was nothing but silence. Most of the crew was asleep.

Loosening the shackles was difficult. It had to be done in the dark, and silently. The iron cut into their wrists and ankles as the spike was forced again and again into the lock's mechanism. Slowly but surely, the men were released.

A woodcut depicting the revolt aboard the Amistad

Each man called the name of the next to take the spike. The captives could hear the scratching of the spike against the ratchet of the iron cuff. Then, one by one, the men announced that they were free.

The first men free went to the crate that held the machetes. They opened it quickly and passed around the long knives. Sengbe knew there wouldn't be time to free all the men before they struck. They would have to take their chances with only a few men. Sengbe took three men with him.

Moving quickly, they silently lifted the hatch cover. They swung themselves up easily onto the deck. The deck was dark and empty—except for the man steering the low schooner into the night wind and the shadows of the Africans moving toward him.

The first scream brought the rest of the *Amistad*'s crew to life. There were frantic shouts, and a lamp was lifted as a white sailor tried to figure out what was happening. The Africans struck furiously, and the crew of the *Amistad*, realizing that their lives were in danger, fought back.

"Throw them some bread!" the captain called out. He knew that the Africans had been half starved. "Throw them some bread!"

Celestino, the cook, stood in front of Sengbe, a loaf of bread in one hand and a long knife in the other. Celestino was struck quickly and fell, mortally wounded.

There was a shot, and then another. Sengbe saw the flash of the muzzle and the captain's face illuminated above it. There were screams as the bullets tore through black flesh. Several men, including Sengbe, moved toward the blazing guns.

It was over quickly. Celestino and the captain were dead. Two white sailors had lowered a small boat over the side of the ship and were rowing furiously away.

Sengbe ordered the Africans to let the white sailors go. They had to secure the ship. He ordered that Ruiz and Montes be brought to him. Montes was shaking as he was pushed in front of Sengbe. Blood was running down the side of his face and onto his shoulder, but he would live. The other man, Jose Ruiz, was unharmed. Sengbe did not want to kill these men. He had seen them steering the boat. He needed them if they were to get back to Africa.

The Africans threw the bodies of Celestino and the captain, Ramon Ferrer, overboard. Sengbe had the men check the ship as best they could. He knew they had to conserve water and food for the long journey.

The Africans waited until the sun rose, as Sengbe had commanded, before making their next move.

Sengbe pointed toward the sun, and then toward the sails of the *Amistad*. They had sailed west from Africa to reach Cuba. Now he wanted the Spaniards to sail in the direction from which the sun had risen—east, to Africa.

The *Amistad* began to sail in a northeasterly direction. Sengbe, by day, could see that the ship was headed east. But at night Montes, who had been a ship's captain at one time, would change the direction of the schooner. The ship first moved toward the Bahamas, and then up the east coast of the United States.

Aboard the ship there was a great deal of worry. The Africans, now free and in charge of the ship, wanted to return to Sierra Leone. But Sengbe knew that it had taken nearly two months to sail from Africa to Cuba. If they were to make the return trip, it would take a lot more supplies than they had.

Sengbe did not know who were his enemies and who were his friends. In Africa, black men had trapped him and sold him into slavery. Pedro Blanco had been white, and so were Ruiz and Montes. Whom could he trust?

Sengbe sent a party of men to shore in a rowboat in the Bahamas.

They brought back some water, but not enough for a long trip. The men were beginning to suffer.

A week passed, and then two. The *Amistad* encountered several ships, but the Africans were wary. Whenever they neared a strange ship, they put the white men belowdecks. But the Africans had no sea experience. Captains on the ships they encountered knew something was wrong. The sails were not properly rigged and the ship flew no flag. Some thought the blacks might have been pirates. After a while newspapers began carrying reports of a "suspicious looking schooner." A steamship was sent out to look for the ship.

The *Amistad* made its way slowly up the east coast of the United States. After a while, Sengbe realized they were no longer headed for Africa. Two Africans had died in the fight to take the ship, killed by Captain Ferrer. Now others looked close to collapse. He needed to get supplies for the trip across the Atlantic. Some of the men tried to drink the saltwater, but it made them violently ill. Montes had a good idea where they were. So did Ruiz. He had been educated in Connecticut and knew about slavery in America and the treatment of American blacks. He felt that if they ran into an American warship, they would be saved.

When the *Amistad* reached Culloden Point on the eastern tip of Long Island, the Africans were in a state of desperation. They couldn't sail up and down the coast forever, and it was clear that they couldn't make it across the ocean to Africa. They needed supplies just to live on while they made more decisions. They dropped anchor and waited, trying to see what was happening on shore. Finally, Sengbe knew they couldn't wait any longer. He decided to lead a party of men to shore. They would take part of the ship's cargo with them to trade. Sengbe got into the rowboat with some men he could trust and headed for the shore.

It was late August and the weather was warm. The land looked peaceful, with tall trees growing not far from the shoreline. There were white men on the shore, but they didn't seem to be alarmed by the sight of the Africans. Sengbe had two men stay with the rowboat while he and the others slowly approached the men on shore. The Africans had the machetes in their belts. Still, none of the white men seemed unduly alarmed.

Two of the men came over to them and spoke. Sengbe didn't understand their language but greeted them in Mande. The exchange went on long enough for Sengbe to sense that the white men, at the very least, were not hostile. He had the trunk they had brought from the ship opened and let the men look into it. There were goods from the *Amistad*'s cargo and a few gold coins. The white men looked carefully at the contents and spoke among themselves.

Sengbe gestured that they wanted food and water. The white men nodded; they understood.

One of the men that they had left with the rowboat ran up to them. Excitedly, he pointed toward the open sea. Sengbe turned to see that a ship had neared the *Amistad*. He started at once for the rowboat.

In seconds, the Africans were rowing toward the schooner. Halfway there they spotted another small boat headed for them, this one filled with men in uniforms. Sengbe told his rowers to turn back toward shore. The men turned the boat around and pulled hard on the oars.

SOUTH HOLLAND PUBLIC LIBRARY

When they reached the shore they abandoned the rowboat and made their way into the bushes. The white men followed.

It was time either to stand and fight or be captured once again. Sengbe hesitated for a long moment. Then one of the sailors lifted his rifle and fired a shot over Sengbe's head. There was no use in trying to fight men who had guns. Sengbe called the Africans out of the bushes, and they laid down their weapons.

They were put back into the rowboat and commanded to row back to the *Amistad.*

CHAPTER 3

Lieutenant Thomas R. Gedney

On Monday, August 26, 1839, the United States brig *Washington* was on patrol between Gardiners Island and Montauk Point. Lieutenant Richard W. Meade spotted what he considered to be a "suspicious looking schooner." Lieutenant Thomas R. Gedney, his superior officer, looked at the ship through his telescope. He turned the scope toward shore and saw a number of people and wagons. He could see that some of the people on shore were black. The schooner's crew, what he could see of it, also appeared to be black.

There were many black sailors aboard ships along the east coast of the United States. African American sailors had fought in the Revolutionary War and the War of 1812. Many free African Americans owned and operated small fishing boats between Philadelphia and Massachusetts. Others worked on whaling ships. But Lt. Gedney had never seen an all-black crew on a schooner the size of the *Amistad*. The idea came to him that the schooner, which had been spotted a number of times in the area, was a smuggler.

An artist's painting of the Amistad

Lt. Gedney had a boat lowered over the side. Lt. Meade and eight other sailors, armed with guns, started rowing toward the *Amistad*. There were no cannons visible on the schooner, so the men would be safe as long as they were in the water; but once they boarded the ship, they had to be ready for anything.

The ship was painted black and green and was built particularly low to the water. The lower half of the schooner was covered with barnacles. A regular ship's captain would not allow that to happen, Lt. Meade thought. The sails were oddly rigged, too, and some were badly torn. Something was desperately wrong. There was no resistance as the sailors boarded the ship. The blacks on deck moved away quickly. Some of them looked sick; several lay on the deck.

Lt. Meade leveled his pistol and signaled all of the blacks to get belowdecks. He wasn't sure what was going on, but he knew he needed to control the situation. He reholstered his pistol and started searching through the cargo strewn about the deck.

Two of the crew of the *Washington* looked belowdecks and a moment later emerged with two white men. The older man's hair was matted to his head.

"Bless the Holy Virgin, you are our preservers!" he exclaimed. He was speaking Spanish.

He started hugging Lt. Meade and wouldn't let go until the officer pulled his revolver again.

Lt. Meade, who spoke Spanish, asked who the captain of the ship was and what flag they were flying under.

Ruiz went into a cabin and produced a Spanish ensign and two letters from his agents, Shelton, Brothers & Co. of Boston and Peter

New London, .Aug. 29, 1839. A card. The subscribers, Don Jose Ruiz and Don Pedro Montez, in gratitude for their most unhoped for and providential rescue from the hands of a ruthless gang of African buccaneers, and an awful death, would take this means of expressing, in some slight degree, their thankfulness and obligation to lieut. T. R. Gedney, and the officers and crew of the U. S. surveying brig Washington, for their decision in seizing the Amistad, and their unremitting kindness and hospitality in providing for their comfort on board their vessel, as well as the means they had taken for the protection of their property.

We also must express our indebtedness to that nation whose flag they so worthily bear, with an assurance that this act will be duly appreciated by our most gracious sovereign her majesty the queen of Spain. **DON JOSE RUIZ.**
DON PEDRO MONTEZ.

This "thank you" note appeared in the Niles National Register.

A. Harmony & Co. of New York. Lt. Meade had his sailors raise the ensign upside down. The incorrectly hung flag would alert Lt. Gedney that there was trouble aboard the ship.

The two Spanish men began to pour out their story. They were businessmen from Cuba. The blacks were slaves which they had bought and were taking to another area of Cuba when, in the middle of the night, the slaves had attacked. They had killed the captain and the cook of the *Amistad* and had taken over the schooner.

After making sure the blacks were locked in the hold, Lt. Meade sent a party to shore to capture the other Africans.

"Their leader is a man named Cinque," Ruiz said. "He's the one who killed the captain."

After a brief skirmish on the shore, the other Africans, including Sengbe (called Cinque by Ruiz), were captured and brought aboard the *Amistad*.

Lt. Meade took the names of the captives. They were listed in the *Niles National Register* of September 7, 1839, as follows:

Cingues, the chief, Quash, Faquorna, Quimboo, Maum, Faa, Gabao, Funny, Pana, Llamani, Guana, Sissi, Con, Sua, Zabry, Paulo Dama, Conorno, Jaoni, Pie, Naquai, Cuba, Baa, Berry, Prummuco, Faha, Huebo, Fuerre, 1st, Fuerre 2nd, Saa, Faguana, Chockamaw, Fasoma, Panguna, Kinna, Carri, Cuperi, Cane, Ferne, Kene, Margra and Antonio Gonzalez.

But Ruiz had a different list of names on an official-looking Spanish document. On this list the names seemed to be of Spanish derivation. The only name that seemed even close on this list was that of Sengbe. His name was listed as Joseph Cinquez.

The Africans on shore were on New York territory, and the Africans aboard the *Amistad* were in the waters off Long Island. But the closest major port was in New London, Connecticut. Lt. Gedney brought his ship alongside the schooner and threw her a line. The schooner was then towed to New London.

CHAPTER 4

The Battle Begins

The battle to end slavery in the United States had been going on for over two hundred years. There were men and women willing to sacrifice their fortunes and even their lives to wipe it out. The fight was led by people such as Anthony Benezet, Prudence Crandall, Frederick Douglass, the Grimké sisters, William Lloyd Garrison, and the brothers Lewis and Arthur Tappan.

Some abolitionists, such as Garrison and later John Brown, believed that constant agitation was necessary. These men said that no law that condemned another man to slavery was valid. The more moderate abolitionists believed that slavery could be ended through the courts and by moral persuasion. These abolitionists looked for opportunities to bring cases to court and to use the media to present the horrors and injustices of slavery to the public.

*Lewis Tappan,
abolitionist*

As news of the *Amistad* affair reached the newspapers, it was read with interest throughout the nation. People who had nothing to do with the actual participants were very much concerned with the outcome and with how the case was being handled. The important questions surrounding the case were listed in the New York *Commercial Advertiser*:

1. Did not the laws of Spain prohibit the slave trade?
2. If Africans were imported into Cuba, wouldn't they be free if the slave trade was not legal?

3. Were there any international agreements which would force the United States to turn over the three little girls to people who said they owned them?

These issues were legal questions. They seemed to suggest that the Africans aboard the *Amistad* should have been free. But there were other issues, too.

In August 1831, in a sleepy community of Southampton County, Virginia, Nat Turner had led a band of slaves who rampaged through the

*Roger S. Baldwin,
chief defense attorney*

*Rev. Simeon S. Jocelyn,
abolitionist*

area, killing their masters and fifty other whites in a bloody rebellion. Although Turner and his band were eventually captured and executed, the uprising had terrified the slaveholders. Some began sleeping with pistols under their pillows. They put tighter controls on slaves. They also tried to keep news of the uprising away from other slaves. The *Amistad* captives had killed at least two people in taking over the ship. Southerners wanted the Africans punished because they had rebelled. They certainly did not want to debate over whether the Africans were free or whether they were entitled to rebel because they had a natural right to freedom.

The Richmond *Enquirer* of September 10, 1839, declared that the government's only duty was to return the blacks to Cuba. But generally the Southern papers were quiet about the incident, maintaining a long-standing policy of not reporting slave rebellions.

At New London a federal marshal was contacted, and on August 29, the marshal arrived at dockside with District Judge Andrew T. Judson. A hearing was conducted aboard the *Washington*.

At the hearing Lt. Gedney told how he had come across the *Amistad*. Then Don Jose Ruiz and Don Pedro Montes told their story.

They said that they were both businessmen based in Cuba, where slavery was legal, as it was in the United States. They had read in the local papers that a large group of *ladinos* were to be sold in Havana. *Ladinos* were African slaves born in Cuba or imported prior to the ban. This was an important point, because importing Africans into Cuba was illegal, but selling slaves or people born into slavery was not. Both Ruiz and Montes said they went to Havana and to the place where the *ladinos* were to be sold, a barracoon called El Misericordia (Mercy). There Don Jose Ruiz said he bought forty-nine of the captives for about $450 each. Don Pedro Montes said he bought four children for about $300 each. They each applied for and received a *traspaso*, a document saying that the slaves they were transporting had not been imported from Africa and were therefore legal. According to Ruiz and Montes, the *ladinos* were then taken aboard the schooner *Amistad*. The names of all the captives were recorded on the *traspaso*, as was the custom.

The ship started out toward southern Cuba, so said the Spaniards, and toward the plantations of Ruiz's family. They ran into bad weather, and the trip, which they had thought would take two days or so, was going badly. On the third night, the slaves escaped from the hold and rushed onto the deck in the darkness. Led by Jose Cinquez, they killed the captain of the ship and the cook.

Since the slaves were part of the cargo, and thus their property, Ruiz and Montes said they simply wanted them returned.

There is reason to believe that Jose Ruiz had never intended to take the captives to Puerto Principe in Cuba, as he had stated in court, but that his actual intent was to bring them into the United States illegally. It is estimated that after the importation of Africans into the United States was outlawed by Congress, thousands of slaves were smuggled into the country each year. In July 1838 an item appeared in *The African Repository*, a publication of the American Colonization Society. It stated that the slave-trading firm owned by Pedro Blanco advised its ship's captains who were engaged in the smuggling of African slaves to always carry a Spanish ensign in case of interception. It also gave a list of agents who would be able to help in case of an emergency. The New York agent was Peter A. Harmony & Co.

When the *Amistad* was boarded by the American naval officers, Ruiz immediately produced the Spanish ensign and the papers identifying his agent as Peter A. Harmony & Co. Harmony is listed in *Longworth's New York Directory* as a merchant whose offices were at 63 Broadway, in lower New York City.

The slave trade, according to British authorities, was conducted out of Havana, where ships would sail for Africa, pick up both Africans and supplies for taking on slaves in Gallinas, then return to Havana. They would then take the Africans to other countries, where they would be smuggled in under cover of darkness. Ruiz and Montes might very well have been intending from the outset to bring the *Amistad* captives into the United States.

In that first hearing aboard the *Washington*, there was no one who could translate the language of the Africans, so their story was not told. Judge Judson ruled that the Africans should be held for trial in federal district court in September 1839.

The Africans were taken to New Haven, Connecticut, where they were placed in the jail run by Colonel Stanton Pendleton. It was actually part jail and part tavern. The Africans proved to be a great curiosity for the town, and people gathered around to look at them as they were brought in.

The four children were taken to a different part of the jail by Mrs. Pendleton. The Africans seemed mild-mannered, even calm. Early reports of them looking like cannibals seemed unfounded. A reporter who went to see them filed this story from Hartford:

I went with some hundreds of others, this morning, to see the captives—paying my entrance fee like an honest man, for the privilege. The nonsense that has been written about them is awful. The sober truth is, that they are just what in the South would be called a likely lot of young Negroes: very few of them seeming to be much if anything over twenty.

They are small, not averaging, I should think, more than five feet and two or three inches. The "cannibal," or "man with the tusks," is a good-tempered-looking fellow, and I venture to say never ate a morsel of man's flesh in his life. Joseph, or Jinqua, or

Shinqua, or Cinquez, is of superior appearance to the rest; indeed he may be called a handsome Negro—with a well-formed head, symmetrical features, and an expression both intelligent and agreeable. When conversing with his fellows, or trying to converse with the white folks, by signs, his look is extremely animated and cheerful, and he gesticulates with great rapidity and variety.

New Haven Herald
September 1839

In New York the case was being studied with interest. The Reverend Joshua Leavitt, a longtime foe of slavery, was selected by a committee of abolitionists to go see the captives. The abolitionists were careful in their selection of causes. Public sympathy was always a strong factor in approaching a case. If the public was on the side of the Africans, even a loss in the courts would create antislavery sentiments.

In New Haven, Rev. Leavitt liked what he saw. Here were intelligent and good-looking men with a particularly striking leader. Even more than that, their case seemed to be legally sound. Leavitt had come to the same opinion that many people in New Haven had reached. The *Amistad* captives, as they were being called, were generally attractive and bright. Public sympathy and curiosity were being aroused. Pendleton, their jailer, was already making money by charging people admission to see the Africans.

The abolitionists Rev. Leavitt, Rev. Simeon Jocelyn, and Lewis Tappan began working to raise money for the defense of the captives. It was Tappan who first located John Ferry, an African who could speak a language that at least some of the *Amistad* captives understood.

Abolitionist mail was often destroyed in the South.

Three lawyers, Seth P. Staples, Theodore Sedgwick, and Roger Baldwin, were hired for their defense. Staples was a New York attorney with an excellent reputation who was willing to donate large portions of his time to a case he believed in. Sedgwick was a young and vigorous lawyer with offices in New York. He had strong antislavery feelings. Baldwin had graduated with honors from Yale University. His mother was the daughter of Roger Sherman, a signer of the Declaration of Independence and a delegate to the Constitutional Convention.

If the captives had landed in another part of the United States—

New Orleans, for example—they might have been treated quite differently. The law was one thing, but how people felt about black people was also important. In 1839 there were few blacks held in slavery in the state of Connecticut, and the feeling of the area was clearly antislavery. New Haven was also a good place for the men of the *Amistad* because of Yale University. Josiah W. Gibbs, a language specialist from Yale, came to visit the men to discover what language they spoke. He knew that there were common ideas expressed by every language. The simplest idea was counting. If Professor Gibbs could get the men to count from one to ten, it would help him find others who spoke their language.

A man capable of the translation was found at the waterfront. James Covey was born in Benderi, in the Mende country. He was captured as a young boy and sold from one place to another until he wound up at Lomboko. After staying at this place for one month, he was put aboard a Portuguese slave ship. The ship, illegally trading in slaves, was captured by a British armed vessel and taken to Sierra Leone. It was in Sierra Leone, the British settlement, that Covey learned English. In November of 1838 he had enlisted aboard the British ship *Buzzard*, commanded by Captain Charles Fitzgerald. The *Buzzard* was an antislavery patroller. When Gibbs approached Covey on the waterfront and started counting in Mande, the Mende language, Covey recognized it at once. Covey also knew another man, Charles Pratt, who spoke the language fluently. Captain Fitzgerald gave Covey leave to translate for the Mende captives. At last the captives would be able to get a full report of the proceedings and, more important, tell their own story.

CHAPTER 5

In the Courts

The *Amistad* captives fought for their freedom when they were first captured. They fought again when they had the chance to take over the *Amistad*. But the most important fight, the one that would determine the fate of the Africans, was the one in the American courts.

September 19, 1839
CIRCUIT COURT OF THE UNITED STATES
Hartford, Connecticut

By the time the federal circuit court opened in September, the publicity around the case had reached a fever pitch. Followers of the case realized its importance not only to the *Amistad* captives but, perhaps, to the very question of slavery in the United States.

The United States government had been requested by the government of Spain to return the *Amistad* captives and to return the *Amistad* and its cargo. The President of the United States, Martin Van Buren, did not want to make an issue of the captives. He was running for reelection and did not want to draw the displeasure of Southern sup-

porters. The simplest decision for the President would be for the court to decide that the *Amistad* captives were slaves and therefore "property," which should be returned under the terms of Pinckney's Treaty. Pinckney's Treaty, signed in 1795, mainly staked out territorial claims between Spain and the United States. But there were also agreements that if a ship from either country were forced into the waters of the other country, the cargo and ship would be returned.

Martin Van Buren, 8th President of the U.S.

If the court decided that the *Amistad* captives were not slaves, and therefore not "property," the position of the government was that the captives should be turned over to the President, who would then see that they were returned to Africa. In either case, it would appear that the President was taking decisive action.

But there were other claims as well. There was maritime law, which concerned conduct and rules of the sea. These laws allowed anyone who rescued a ship in distress or who performed a service to a ship in distress to make a claim for salvage rights, those rights being a part of the value of the ship and its cargo. In the case of the *Amistad*, two such claims were being made. One was being made by Lt. Gedney of the *Washington*. He claimed that he rescued the *Amistad* and its cargo and was therefore entitled to a portion of its value.

When the *Amistad* captives went ashore, they were met by Henry Green and four of his friends. Green claimed that he had been about to rescue the ship and its crew. Gedney took command of the operation, but, Green claimed, his intent entitled him to a portion of the value.

Don Pedro Montes claimed that the four children, valued at $1,200, were his property and should be returned to him.

At this point in the proceedings, no formal charges had been made against the *Amistad* captives.

The lawyers for the captives had two basic goals. The first was to show the Africans as human beings. They didn't want them to be referred to as "slaves" or to appear as beings different from the judge and other people involved in the case. The second goal was to make the law work for them and not just against them. The lawyers understood that the case would be somewhat like a chess game, with each side trying to outmaneuver the other. The first move by the defense was to apply for a writ of habeas corpus.

One of the strongest points in American law is the writ of habeas corpus. The Latin words *habeas corpus* mean "you should have the body." If a person is arrested in the United States, the courts must, within a reasonable time, bring a legal reason for holding the person. This prevents people from being held in prison without a trial. The defense asked for a writ of habeas corpus for the three girls, who were between the ages of seven and nine. Teme had lived in Africa with her mother, older brother, and sister. Kague was one of nine children. Both of her parents had been alive when men broke into her home and made them prisoners. Margru was seven years old.

The fourth child was a precocious little boy named Kali. The defense, however, thought that the girls would excite more sympathy.

The girls were brought crying into the courtroom, afraid of what might happen to them, holding desperately to the matron who had been in charge of them in prison. They had every right to be frightened. They had been taken from their homes, sold into slavery, made to cross the Atlantic Ocean in the hold of a slave ship, seen their fellow Africans beaten and starved, seen the mutiny aboard the *Amistad,* and now were in an American prison.

Theodore Sedgwick opened the argument for habeas corpus by saying that the girls had been taken in the slave trade, which was against the laws of Spain, and therefore they were not "slaves" or "property" but three young girls being illegally held.

The prosecuting attorney, Ralph Ingersoll, argued that the girls were being held by the district court and that the district court should resolve its issues before the circuit court made a decision.

The United States is divided into legal districts, and each has its court system. People are tried in district courts for crimes, or they can bring legal cases against each other. Circuit courts are courts of appeal, where a party can appeal legal questions. The defense team was appealing the right of any court to hold the girls without a formal charge. In the meantime, a grand jury was being held to determine if the adult *Amistad* captives should be tried for murder or mutiny.

Before a citizen of the United States is put on trial for a crime, he or she must first be indicted by a grand jury. The grand jury decides if there is sufficient reason to believe that the accused person might have committed the crime. If so, the person will stand trial. If the grand jury says that there is not sufficient reason to believe the person has committed a crime, then the person must be freed.

The first victory for the defense came when Judge Smith Thompson, after hearing the facts brought before the grand jury by the prosecutor, declared that the captives could not be tried for murder or piracy. Whatever had happened, his ruling went, it had happened on a Spanish ship and in international waters. The United States government had no right to try people for crimes that had not happened in the United States or to citizens of the United States.

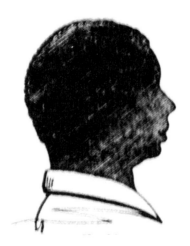

Silhouettes of the captives: Foone, Burna, and Shuma

Roger Baldwin, perhaps heartened by the decision that the captives would not be tried for murder or piracy, continued to argue for habeas corpus. He said:

> What are the facts? What are the probable grounds on which the claim of property in these individuals is set up? Here are three children, between the ages of seven and nine years, who are proved to be native Africans, who cannot speak our own language or the Spanish language, or any other but the language of their nativity. Does this honorable Court see they cannot be slaves? They were not born slaves, they were born in Africa. Are we to set aside our own laws, and those of every civilized nation, who have long held this trade to be piratical and infamous?

Baldwin was arguing that the slave trade was illegal and that the three little girls could not have been born into slavery. But his argument also suggested that the girls could not be property because they were persons. In 1839 the United States and Spain allowed slavery to exist within their borders. In other words, in parts of the United States, Connecticut included, a human being could have the status of "property" by being a slave, and therefore would not be counted as a "person." Ralph Ingersoll was quick to point this out:

> Again, we have been told that these persons cannot be considered as property, because this is a free country. We are before a court acting for a peculiar kind of government. In a part of these states, slaves are

recognized as property. It is idle for the gentleman to stand here and say they are persons and therefore not property.

Defense lawyer Seth Staples pleaded:

> Go on with your litigation, as to the *Amistad* and her cargo, to your heart's content, but take not these children and deprive them of the habeas corpus, under a pretext of a question whether they are brutes or human beings!

The argument here goes to the heart of the case. Natural law, the law that seems natural to the human condition, says that all men are born free and cannot lose that freedom unless they have committed a crime and are tried and convicted. But positive law, the law a society makes, said in 1839 that some people were not born free and might lose their freedom if the law so stated. How were the *Amistad* captives to be treated? If they had been white, it is clear that natural law would have prevailed. But they were Africans.

The defense also wanted the case moved from Connecticut to New York. Since slavery was illegal in New York, the defense team felt it had a better chance of winning the freedom of the captives there.

William Hungerford, representing the claims of Ruiz and Montes, continued to view the girls as property and said they should be returned to the Spaniards under Pinckney's Treaty.

If the girls were declared property by the court, the ruling might still have been against restoring them under this treaty. Pinckney's

Treaty settled a border dispute in 1795 between the United States and Spain. Within the treaty certain agreements were made about ships of the respective nations. Added to the treaty were agreements about ships owned by citizens of Spain or the United States. It said that if one of these ships entered the waters of the other country under distress, the ships and cargoes would be respected and restored to the rightful owners.

On Monday, September 23, Judge Thompson gave his rulings on the case. He first denied habeas corpus to the girls. He said further that the issue before the circuit court was to simply determine the jurisdiction of the district court. Judge Thompson went on to say that he had to obey the laws of the United States, not just the laws of a particular district, and that, because the laws of the United States allow the right of property in persons, in slaves, then the case could be decided with that question in mind. It was not clear, however, if the District of Connecticut or the District of New York had jurisdiction.

The hearings in the circuit court were then closed. Immediately upon the closing of the circuit court, the district court, under Judge Andrew T. Judson, was opened. To determine jurisdiction, Judson directed that an investigation be made as to exactly where the *Amistad* had been taken. He allowed bail to be set for the captives according to their value as slaves. He then adjourned the court until the third Tuesday in November.

The bail that was allowed—according to the value of the Africans as slaves—was not acceptable to the defense team. The defense would not accept this reference to their clients as property. The Africans were remanded again to the jail in New Haven.

The *Amistad* captives would not be charged with murder, but they were still not free. Judge Thompson had also kept open the possibility, in his ruling denying habeas corpus, that the captives might be found to be property.

The United States was a young country, barely fifty years old, when the case opened. Its laws, especially the laws affecting people of African descent, were often not clear. Natural law, those laws that seem morally right to most people, sometimes applied to blacks and

Ruiz and Montes were taken to this newly built prison in downtown New York.

sometimes did not. In many instances, positive law, the laws made by national or state governments, took from blacks the rights most people consider basic. The defense team felt that an appeal to natural law would aid their case. They wanted to paint a portrait of Ruiz and Montes as evil men. They also wanted to keep the case before the public. They filed lawsuits on behalf of Sengbe and Fulah, another of the captives, charging Ruiz and Montes with assault and unlawful imprisonment. Lewis Tappan himself accompanied the sheriff as they served the papers on the two Cubans in New York City. The arrests made instant headlines.

In 1839 in the United States, it was exceedingly rare for a black man to serve legal papers on a white man. The nature of the charges, that the men were assaulted and illegally imprisoned, brought the matter to a fever pitch. Weren't there millions of people of African descent in the United States who could claim that either they or their parents or grandparents had been assaulted and illegally held? Slavery was hardly a volunteer institution!

The New York *Advertiser & Express* wondered, in an editorial comment on October 19, if the next step wouldn't be "the arrest and imprisonment of Southern gentlemen traveling in the Northern States at the suit of their own servants."

Of course, nothing would have pleased the abolitionists more. It also produced discomfit in the White House. President Van Buren saw that he had considerably less influence in the case of the *Amistad* captives than did the abolitionists.

At a hearing, Ruiz and Montes were allowed to post bail. Ruiz's bail was reduced to $250 and Montes was allowed to leave on his own recognizance. Ruiz refused to put up the bail and went to jail in the newly built Tombs in lower New York City. The jail was not at all uncomfortable. He could send out for food and had what would be considered luxury accommodations. Ruiz spent a total of four months in the New York jail. Montes, once released from the hearing, returned to Cuba as soon as possible with no intention of returning.

November 19, 1839
DISTRICT COURT
Hartford, Connecticut

When the trial in the district court began, the defense again asked for a change in jurisdiction. They felt that Judge Judson would not be sympathetic to the *Amistad* captives and also that it would be better to have the trial in a state in which slavery was illegal. But after listening to the testimony of Green, Gedney, and the other participants in the taking of the *Amistad*, Judge Judson decided that the case could be tried in Connecticut. What he determined was that the ship had been taken in the ocean, and although some of the captives had been on land, they were still attached to the ship.

When regular testimony began, the two sides repeated their positions as to the state of the captives. Judge Judson listened as lawyers for Ruiz and Montes insisted that the Africans were legally slaves. The lawyers for the *Amistad* captives insisted they were not slaves at all, but free Africans kidnapped from their homes.

James Covey, who had been translating for the captives, was ill.

The defense asked for a postponement so that the story of the captives could be heard. When Judge Judson found that several of the other attorneys could not stay, he allowed a postponement until January 7, 1840, and agreed to take the testimony of a defense witness, Dr. Richard Robert Madden, later that afternoon. Dr. Madden, who had spent years in Cuba monitoring the slave trade, testified that many Africans were being brought into Cuba, in violation of Spanish law but with the cooperation of the Cuban officials.

Meanwhile, the captives were being kept in Pendleton's jail in New Haven. Since it was ruled that they would not be charged with murder or piracy, they were given more freedom. They were allowed out onto the New Haven green, where they would exercise. The captives were quite good at doing somersaults. This amused the crowds, and soon people were coming from miles away to see them.

Sengbe did not like being put on display. When Colonel Pendleton allowed people into the jail to see the captives, Sengbe felt humiliated. They weren't animals to be looked at by curious crowds, they were human beings.

Several black abolitionists also took an interest in the case. Among them were Reverend James W. C. Pennington of Hartford and Robert Purvis. Purvis, a successful businessman, asked the artist Nathaniel Jocelyn to consider doing a portrait of Sengbe.

Other artists came to the New Haven jail to sketch the Africans. There were wax masks made of them. Their heads were measured by phrenologists, people who believed that the shape of the head indicated character and intelligence. They had, in fact, become celebri-

Nathaniel Jocelyn's stirring portrait of Sengbe Pieh

ties. Few Americans knew much about blacks, especially blacks who had never known slavery or oppression. They were fascinated by these people.

The four children were given instruction in reading, writing, and religion, and they seemed to be fast learners.

The trial resumed on January 7. The same arguments were being offered. But on Wednesday, January 8, while Professor Gibbs was on the stand discussing the language of the captives to prove that they were Africans and not Spanish, Judge Judson made a ruling that surprised everyone. He said that he was "fully convinced that the men are recently from Africa, and it is idle to deny it."

The courtroom was stunned. Students from Yale University Law School, released from classes to hear the proceedings, buzzed among themselves and took furious notes. Professor Gibbs continued his testimony concerning the meaning of the names of the captives, but the spectators were already trying to figure the impact of the judge's decision. Gibbs gave testimony that the language of the captives was Mande, not Spanish. He had learned that all of the Mende names were consistent with African, not Spanish, customs. Then, finally, it was time for Sengbe to give his testimony.

It was a cold day and Sengbe had a blanket around his shoulders, which he wore like a royal robe. The students from Yale, visiting lawyers, businessmen, clergymen—all the people who had been so fascinated by the case—now leaned eagerly forward. Covey, the young African, came forward with Sengbe to translate.

Sengbe stood tall, giving the impression that he could be as tall as he wanted to be, and began his tale. He told how he had been captured by slavers, how he had been taken to Lomboko and sold.

The ship that he had been put upon was packed with its human cargo, and Sengbe crouched upon the floor to show how they were forced to lie one next to the other. He brought his hands and his feet together to show how the Africans had been manacled.

Through the interpreter, he stated that Burna had been viciously beaten. Ruiz had ordered the man whipped for taking more water than he should have, Sengbe said.

There were not more than two people in the crowded courtroom who could understand Sengbe directly, but they were all captivated by his presence and by the fire in his voice and face. When he had finished answering questions, he made a passionate plea.

"He is asking for freedom," Covey said.

From the audience there was light applause. And then, lifting his arms to the onlookers, Sengbe called out in English.

"Give us free!" Sengbe called. "Give us free!"

On January 13, having heard all of the testimony, Judge Judson gave his verdict. The major part of his verdict said that Lt. Gedney was entitled to salvage and that Ruiz and Montes could also claim part of the cargo and value of the ship. The captives had not been slaves, the judge declared, and would not be forced to return to the custody of the Spanish. But they had been brought into the United States as slaves, which was illegal. They would therefore be turned over to the President of the United States to be returned to Africa.

Judson had clearly misread the law. The law stated that if Africans were intentionally brought into the United States to be slaves, then they would be returned by the President. The *Amistad* captives had brought themselves into the United States.

Judson also said that Antonio, who had been owned by Ramon Ferrer, the slain captain of the *Amistad*, was a slave and should be returned to the Spanish.

The abolitionists had wanted more. They had wanted the Africans to be absolutely free to do as they pleased. But the captives weren't going to be sent back to the Spanish, so the case was considered a victory. The *Amistad* captives were free of the threat of becoming slaves and were to be returned to Africa.

But it was not to be that simple.

Decisions made in district courts can be appealed. The circuit court would be meeting in April, and the United States district attorney filed an appeal on two counts. The Spanish government wanted the blacks returned. They were also appealing the salvage granted to Lt. Gedney and the two Spaniards.

In May the case was brought before Judges Thompson and Judson in the circuit court. Judge Thompson affirmed the lower court's ruling pro forma (as a matter of formality). He understood that no matter what the circuit court ruled, the case would be appealed to the Supreme Court. By simply affirming the lower court's ruling, he allowed the case to go directly to the Supreme Court.

For the *Amistad* captives, the wait was almost unbearable. They had been told of the decision of the district court and had thought they were free. Now they had to go through another long delay and another possibility that they would be forced into slavery.

The United States Supreme Court is the court of last appeal.

CHRONICLE.

THE AMISTAD. In pursuance of a decree of the circuit court, this famous vessel, together with her cargo, was, on Thursday last, sold by auction, under the direction of the marshal of the district, at the custom house in this city. An appraisal was had of vessel and cargo when the goods were first landed. We understand that the amount of that appraisal was about six thousand six hundred dollars, and that the gross sales will amount to within four or five hundred dollars of that sum.

The vessel was valued by the appraisers at $600, and sold for only $245. She is of some fifty or sixty tons burden, built in Cuba, and said to be old. Her sails are all worn to shreds, and a large expenditure would be necessary to render her sea worthy.

[*New London Republican.*

The sale of the Amistad. *The paper is wrong about where it was built.*

There are no higher courts or other recourses. Both sides knew that the battle on the Supreme Court level would be final.

The Supreme Court has nine members, but one justice was too ill to hear the case. Another justice, Judge Smith Thompson, had already heard the arguments. The arguments before the Supreme Court would not be different from the arguments that had been before the lower courts. But would the Supreme Court justices see the case the same way?

The defense approached several prominent lawyers to join them in their presentation of the *Amistad* case. Again they wanted to keep the case in the public eye, and a high-profile attorney would do that. Also, the defense team was worried that the decision to send the

John Quincy Adams

Amistad captives back to Cuba would be easier if the case was seen to be simply the abolitionist cause versus the United States government. The agitation that worked so well in keeping the case public and argued over could work against them in front of the Supreme Court. They needed an attorney whose stature would elevate the case.

John Quincy Adams had followed the case closely. He had written several letters to the defense team advising them on points of law. Adams had been the sixth president of the United States and a member of the State Department when Pinckney's Treaty had been ratified in 1795. His father, John Adams, had been the second president of the United States, succeeding George Washington. Baldwin, Staples, and Sedgwick, the rest of the defense team, were younger, but the prestige of Adams would lift their stature considerably. He was asked to join the defense, and he agreed to do so.

But Adams hadn't tried a case in more than thirty years. He was over seventy years old, and he often had to hold his hands to keep them from shaking involuntarily. Many thought he would be unable to stand the ordeal of a long Supreme Court presentation. But Adams was also a fighter.

The Adams name was highly respected, and the press, who were increasingly attacking the abolitionists, were not so eager to attack a man whose family had helped found the country. The addition of Adams brought new hope to the captives. Kali, now about ten years old, wrote a letter to the ex-president. He had clearly learned a lot of English.

Dear Friend Mr. Adams,

I want to write a letter to you because you love Mendi people, and you talk to the grand court. We want to tell you one thing. Jose Ruiz say we born in Havana, he tell lie. We all born in Mendi.

We want you to ask the Court what we have done wrong. What for Americans keep us in prison? Some people say Mendi people crazy; Mendi people dolt; because we no talk American language. Merica people no talk Mendi language; Merica people dolt?

They tell bad things about Mendi people, and we no understand. Some men say Mendi people very happy because they laugh and have plenty to eat. Mr. Pendleton come, and Mendi people all look sorry because they think about Mendi land and friends we no see now. Mr. Pendleton say Mendi people angry;

Kali

white men afraid of Mendi people. The Mendi people no look sorry again—that why we laugh. But Mendi people feel sorry; O, we can't tell how sorry. Some people say Mendi people no got souls. Why we feel bad we no got souls?

Dear friend Mr. Adams, you have children, you have friends, you love them, you feel sorry if Mendi people come and carry them all to Africa. We feel bad for our friends, and our friends all feel bad for us. If American people give us free we glad, if they no give us free we sorry—we sorry for Mendi people little, we sorry for American peo-ple great deal, because God punish liars. We want you to tell court that Mendi people no want to go back to Havana, we no want to be killed. Dear Friend, we want you to know how we feel, Mendi people think, think, think. Nobody know what we think; the teacher he know, we tell him some. Mendi people have got souls. All we want is make us free.

The case opened on February 22, 1841. Henry D. Gilpin opened for the plaintiffs. His arguments went over the same claims, that the Africans were slaves, and under the treaty of 1795 they should be returned to Spain.

Roger Baldwin and John Quincy Adams pleaded for the captives. Baldwin attacked the case on the legal issues, that the Africans had been brought into Cuba illegally; that they were not, and never were, slaves; and that they were entitled to be free. Adams argued the moral issues, emphasizing that the United States was a land of jus-tice, and justice demanded the freedom of the captives.

There was a brief break in the case due to the death of Justice

Philip P. Barbour, who had died in his sleep on February 24. The trial was resumed the following Monday, March 1.

When testimony continued, the arguments of the government lawyers focused on the need for the United States to honor its treaties. The defense lawyers listened and wondered what the judges were thinking. Many of the judges were from the South, where slavery was well entrenched. Chief Justice Roger B. Taney, from Maryland, was considered a Southern sympathizer.

Some onlookers wondered if the arguments of John Quincy Adams had

Roger B. Taney, Chief Justice of the Supreme Court

been effective. He had broadened the fight but had not attacked the government's case as neatly as Roger Baldwin had. When the arguments were closed, some abolitionists worried that they might lose the case.

March 9, 1841
SUPREME COURT
Washington, D.C.

When it was announced that the Supreme Court was ready to read its decision, the air was full of tension. For Sengbe, Grabeau, Foone, Kali, and even little Teme, it could mean a life of slavery or even death. There were no hints to ease the blow of a bad decision; there was no place to appeal. Representatives of the Spanish and American governments were present at the reading of the decision by Justice Joseph Story.

The decision was clear and powerful. The arguments of the government on behalf of Spain and on behalf of Ruiz and Montes were rejected. The Africans, Justice Story declared, had never been slaves under international law and had been taken illegally from their native lands. They were, therefore, to go free. This was the same decision that the lower courts had made. But the Supreme Court rejected the idea that the captives should be turned over to the President of the United States to be returned to Africa. Under the laws of the United States, Africans intentionally brought into the United States for the slave trade were to be returned by the President. There had been no evidence presented that the Africans had been intentionally brought into the country to be made slaves in this country.

As to the taking over of the *Amistad*, the Supreme Court ruled that the Africans had the "ultimate right of all human beings in extreme cases to resist oppression, and to apply force against ruinous injustice."

In 1841 there was no television or radio. It took two days for the

Justice Joseph Story

news of the decision to travel from Washington, D.C., to New York City, where it was published. It was then sent to New Haven by steamboat. The captives were being held in Westville, Connecticut. United States Marshal Norris Wilcox went by stagecoach out to the jail in Westville to inform the Africans of the result of the trial.

Wilcox gave the Africans the newspaper announcing the Supreme Court decision, and Sengbe had the boy Kali read it aloud. Sengbe still wasn't sure that they were really free, but soon the abolitionists involved in the case began to arrive, and the celebrating began in earnest.

For the first time in over two years, the *Amistad* captives were free.

CHAPTER 6

What Is Freedom?

When word came to the *Amistad* captives that the Supreme Court had declared them free, they were elated but still wary. They had not been bad people in Africa, and yet they had been captured for the slave trade. They had seen no justification for their being put into chains and sold to Pedro Blanco, and yet that, too, had happened.

The experience in Cuba was just as bitter. The thirty-seven men and four children who had survived the journey had been starved, some had been beaten, and all had despaired of their chances of ever being free again. On the *Amistad* they had struck a blow for their own freedom, only to fall into the hands of the Americans, who had put them through almost two years of trials and uncertainty. For the Africans, the Americans had no more right to determine their freedom than Pedro Blanco or Jose Ruiz.

Being free meant that they could return to their homes in Africa, but that would cost money. The *Tecora*, the ship that had brought them from Africa to Cuba, had been manned by an entire crew of experienced sailors. The ship had been provisioned with food and water for both the crew and the African captives. But the attempt to go back to Africa on the *Amistad* showed the captives that without sufficient food and water, they would never make it. In a way, even though released from the jail in Connecticut, they were still captives.

The abolitionists understood that there were still dangers for the Africans. Their English was still, in most cases, not good enough to allow them to earn a living. There were also people more than willing to take advantage of them.

The three girls—Teme, Margru, and Kague—had been living in the Pendleton home. The abolitionists claimed that the girls were being forced to work for practically nothing and were almost slaves. The girls said they wanted to stay with the Pendletons. But they had been so mistreated for so much of their lives that almost any stable home was better than what they had been through.

Besides needing the money for a ship back to Sierra Leone, the Africans also needed time to decide what they wanted to do with the rest of their lives. The area from which they had come, near the Gallinas River, was still a dangerous one. Slave ships still visited the shores looking for fresh bodies to carry across the ocean. Many of the Africans freed by antislavery patrols and returned to the shore areas were recaptured and put into slavery again within weeks.

The abolitionists had their own plans. They understood the popularity of the *Amistad* captives and knew that they could attract more people to their cause by using them. They also wanted to give the Africans training in becoming Christians.

To maintain their influence over them, the abolitionists decided to house the captives away from the site of all the publicity in New Haven. The place chosen was Farmington, Connecticut. The men agreed to go, and the three girls, after a court hearing in which the Pendletons tried to keep them, also moved reluctantly to the central Connecticut town.

Farmington had been a farming community for hundreds of years. Before English colonists moved into the area, it had been farmed by Indians. There were many abolitionists there, as well as many houses that had been stops on the Underground Railroad.

The Underground Railroad was a network of roads and houses that were friendly to runaway slaves. In some houses in Farmington, the runaways could get directions and perhaps food. Other places often had secret rooms or secret shelters in which the fleeing blacks could hide. One such stop on the Underground Railroad was the home of Samuel Deming.

Deming, one of the leading citizens of Farmington, owned a small general store in the heart of the city. When the *Amistad* men arrived in mid-March, he volunteered to let them stay in the room above the store. It was there, while a more suitable place was being built, that the men lived and went to school for six days each week. The store is small, and the men were sleeping and living very close to each other, but it was better than the New Haven prison. Kali stayed with the men.

The three girls, now between nine and eleven, lived with private families. Margru lived in the Porters' house. Reverend Noah Porter was a wealthy man and a strong believer in education. The Porter family felt it their Christian duty to treat all people equally.

The Farmington store where the captives were housed still stands.

Teme lived with the Johnson family. A quiet girl, she planted pineapples and cared for the Johnsons' garden.

Kague lived in the Cowleses' home, a stop on the Underground Railroad.

Many of the townspeople were against slavery but also against the abolitionists. They looked at people like Lewis Tappan and Samuel Deming as troublemakers. They weren't sure about suddenly having a group of Africans living in their community. The abolitionists felt that if the people of Farmington met the *Amistad* captives, they would change their minds. So it was that a group of the Africans, including Sengbe, marched into a church service at the First Church of Christ, Congregational. The church, organized in 1652, is an inspir-

Interior of church

The First Church of Christ, Congregational

Barracks built by abolitionist Austin F. Williams

ing building. The tower is a landmark that can be seen from miles away. The interior of the building is spare and elegant and must have been awesome to the Africans. At the time, the members of the church were, of course, familiar with the case. The parishioners opened their hearts to the captives, as did most of the people in Farmington. The men had only the shirts and pants they had been given in the New Haven jail, and women who could sew volunteered to make clothing for them. The girls, all of whom were quite small, were given clothing collected from the church members. The dresses they wore proudly, but they took the shawls and made them into turbans.

Austin F. Williams had a long reputation as an abolitionist. He had entertained the idea of helping the Africans escape if they had lost in court. Now he hired a company to build lodging for the captives. An airy dwelling was built on Williams's property. It provided plenty of room for all of the men. The cost of the lodging was over

The barracks were made to accommodate a large group.

$400, and Williams hoped to use it as a carriage house after the Africans left.

While most of the people of Farmington had no problems with the Mende men, there were some who resented them. They were used to American blacks, many of whom were different than the Mende. As the courts had made clear, the Mende had never been slaves. They had never been made to feel uncomfortable about skin color. Some people in Farmington resented these black people, and there were a few incidents of fighting. Williams tried to keep the *Amistad* captives away from the townspeople to avoid problems.

When the Mende were not being taught at the church, they often worked on a fifteen-acre site they were allowed to use for farming. The men also realized that the people in Farmington liked to see them do the calisthenics and somersaults that they could do so well. But now the Africans charged for their performances.

Sengbe appreciated the kindness shown to him by the abolitionists, but he was far from satisfied. He disliked the idea of the Africans being kept away from the townspeople. He mentioned this to John Norton, a Farmington resident and supporter of the men. Norton, a particularly kindly man, was the one the Africans most often turned to when they were troubled.

In the jail in New Haven, the Africans had had almost as much freedom as they now had in Farmington. They were confined to the

Acreage farmed by the Amistad *captives in Farmington*

barracks much of the time. Other times Sengbe and some of the others were taken to lectures as the abolitionists tried to raise money for their passage back to Africa. Sengbe did not like being put on display. He realized that many of the whites looking at him thought of him as an oddity, rather than as a man who deserved freedom as fully as they. The Reverend J. W. C. Pennington welcomed them in his church in Hartford and they did feel comfortable there.

As the summer wore on, the money to hire a ship and crew for the return to Africa slowly came in. There weren't many black people in Farmington, and there was little chance for a social life. A black woman who ran a boardinghouse, Mrs. Freeman, was hired to cook for them, and she tried to learn to cook the way they had been used to in Sierra Leone.

Increasingly, the feeling of freedom was slipping away from the Africans. True, they were free of the chains that had been fastened around their ankles and wrists when they were first captured. They were also free from the jail in New Haven. But they were still trapped in the role of being different. They longed for a life in which they would not be stared at or forced to tell their stories over and over again to raise money. The *Amistad* captives, as they were still called in the press, realized that they were on the margins of American life. More and more they were being treated like other American blacks. They were sometimes referred to as savages. On some of the trips they were not allowed to sit with white passengers on trains.

They understood, too, that they were still living in a country where many of the people who had black skin were slaves. They could not feel comfortable knowing they were free only because a court had decided that they were. The people they saw did not always agree that they should be free. Some of the captives felt that the abolitionists wanted them to stay in the United States to further the cause of freedom in this country. That was fine for the abolitionists, but the Africans needed to be able to have their own lives and their own struggles. When it was suggested that they return to Africa and start a special Mende mission, they agreed. But when could they go?

The Supreme Court decision had been announced in March. In August, one of the *Amistad* captives, a man known as Foone, was swimming in the canal basin. A rice planter in Sierra Leone, he had left his family to go to the rice fields one day when he was captured and sold into slavery. Foone was known to be a good swimmer, as were all the Africans in this group, but he was also depressed from being apart from his wife and family. He had at one time seemed the most lighthearted of the men and was a great favorite among the people in both New Haven and Farmington.

On Saturday, August 7, two years after the captives had been on the *Amistad* off the coast of New York, Foone's body floated in the basin.

Sengbe ran to the Norton home with the news that Foone was dead. He said the words with tears in his eyes and despair in his face. Foone was buried in Riverside Cemetery. Austin F. Williams wrote to Lewis Tappan that he thought the African man, homesick and filled with gloom, had committed suicide. The Africans had to be returned to their home soon.

The abolitionists stepped up their efforts to raise money, and finally a ship was engaged. Then it was only a matter of finding men and

The river basin where Foone drowned

women to go with them to help build a Christian mission in Sierra Leone. By building such a mission, the Africans would be a living memorial to the justice they had received in the American courts.

The Reverend and Mrs. William Raymond agreed to go to Sierra Leone and stay for several years to help establish the mission. The abolitionists wanted a black minister to go with them and asked Rev.

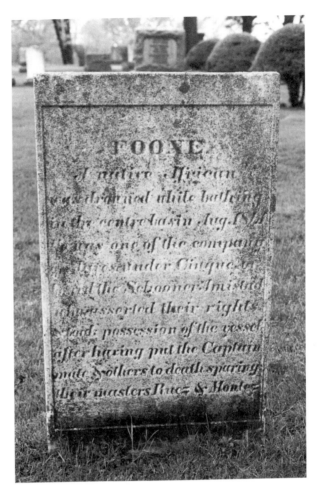

Foone's tombstone in Farmington cemetery

Pennington, who himself had escaped from slavery, to go to Africa. Rev. Pennington thanked the abolitionists for the chance to go to Africa, but he said he thought he would serve his people better in the United States.

Finally two other couples were found. The Reverend and Mrs. James Steele and Mr. and Mrs. Henry Wilson agreed to go.

On November 17, the Africans attended a last church service and headed toward New York. After a round of farewells, the Africans and the missionaries boarded the ship *Gentleman*. On November 25, 1841, they began their journey home.

In the middle of January 1842, they arrived in Freetown, Sierra Leone. Africa at last, and free at last!

Epilogue

The return of the *Amistad* captives to Africa was truly remarkable. In a time when slavery was legal in the United States, free men put their time, fortunes, and reputations on the line to protect the freedom of these men and children. "Justice," said John Quincy Adams, "is the will to secure to everyone his own right."

Slavery was not ended, but the efforts of many people—the abolitionists; the people of New Haven, Farmington, and New York; as well as students and teachers from Yale—brought the plight of all people of African descent into sharp focus. The real conflict between those natural rights of which Thomas Jefferson speaks in the Declaration of Independence and the positive laws that allowed people to be enslaved was not settled until the end of the Civil War. But the victory of those who struggled so that the *Amistad* captives could go free brought more and more people into that struggle to secure freedom for all.

Perhaps the most important aspect of the efforts of Lewis Tappan, Austin F. Williams, Joshua Leavitt, the other abolitionists, as well as the attorneys involved was that they allowed the world to see the Africans as human beings.

Hale Woodruff's 1939 Mural of the Amistad *Rebellion. This panel shows the return to Africa.*

And what of the Africans themselves? In account after account of Sengbe Pieh, called Cinque or Cinquez by the press, we are given the impression of a man whose very presence was outstanding. Artists drew him. Journalists wrote about him. College professors brought their students to see him. Of all the *Amistad* captives, his was the only name that Don Jose Ruiz seemed to know.

The significance of the *Amistad* captives was not lost on the thousands of slaveholders in the United States. It was people like Sengbe, they knew, who could bring the practice of slavery to bloody conflict. And yet Sengbe as a free man was not violent. He sang with the other captives in Lewis Tappan's church. He turned somersaults on the New Haven green. During the entire proceedings, he maintained a quiet dignity.

Sengbe was grateful for all the help he received in this country, and especially from the man he considered a king, John Quincy Adams.

To the Honorable John Quincy Adams,
Most respected Sir.—The Mendi people give you thanks
for all your kindness to them. They will never forget
your defence of their rights before the great Court at
Washington. They feel that they owe to you, in a large
measure, their deliverance from the Spaniards, and
from slavery or death. They will pray for you as long

as they live, Mr. Adams. May God bless and reward you.

We are about to go home to Africa. We go to Sierra Leone first, and then we reach Mendi very quick.—When we get to Mendi we will tell the people of your great kindness. Good missionary will go with us. We shall take the Bible with us. It has been a precious book in prison, and we love to read it now we are free! Mr. Adams, we want to make you a present of a beautiful Bible. Will you please accept it and when you look at it or read it, remember your poor and grateful clients? We read in this Holy Book, "If it had not been the Lord who was on our side, when man rose up against us, then they had swallowed us up quick, when their wrath was kindled against us. Blessed be the Lord who hath not given us as a prey to their teeth. Our soul is escaped as a bird out of the snare of the fowler; the snare is broken and we are escaped. Our help is in the name of the Lord who made heaven and Earth.

For the Mendi people,
CINQUE, KINNA, KA-LE

On the other hand, even in the brief time they were in the United States, the captives were subjected to racial prejudice.

What happened to the *Amistad* captives after their return to Africa? Things went badly for them. Many, including Sengbe, found that their families had either been killed or sold into slavery. The Mendi Mission near Freetown, Sierra Leone, had money problems, and it was difficult to maintain over the years.

Teme remained a Christian and lived for a while at the mission.

Margru, as a young woman, attended Oberlin College.

Writing in *The Farmington Magazine*, Mr. Johnson, with whom she had stayed, remembered her as a little girl and "how happy working in his little garden had made her."

Margru, who had been baptized Sarah Kinson while in Farmington, returned to the United States five years later. In August 1846, she began studies at Oberlin College in Ohio. She expressed a desire to better herself so as to be a useful person in society and to be able to teach others. After studying at Oberlin, she returned to Sierra Leone, using her skills to educate African children.

Kague, who had been baptized in Farmington and given the Christian name of Charlotte, died in Sierra Leone of malaria in 1847.

Kali, the young boy who had written the moving letter to John Quincy Adams, became attached to Rev. Raymond and worked with

him in Africa. In his later years, Pa Raymond, as he was called, was a much-loved and respected member of the mission.

All was not as the abolitionists had hoped. Many of the *Amistad* captives returned to African ways and African religions, as they had returned to the African continent. But Sengbe and the *Amistad* captives were free. Their lives were what they could make of them, as are the lives of all free people. It is what Sengbe had asked, to be "given *free*."

Amistad captive Kali in later life

At the end of his life, Sengbe returned to the mission and worked as an interpreter. He died at the mission in 1879.

CREDITS

Title page, pp. 9, 36–37, 63: the New Haven Colony Historical Society; pp. 10–12, 18–19: *Illustrated London News*; pp. 17, 69, 93, endpapers: Beinecke Rare Book and Manuscript Library, Yale University; p. 25: Irungu Mutu; pp. 27, 94: Mission Album Collection, United Methodist Church Archives, Madison, N.J.; pp. 28–29, 42, 44, 49, 73: Library of Congress; p. 43: Baldwin Family Papers, Manuscript and Archives, Yale University Library; p. 52: National Portrait Gallery, Smithsonian Institution/Art Resource, N.Y.; p. 59: copyright © Collections of the New-York Historical Society; p. 68: Metropolitan Museum of Art; pp. 90–91: Talladega College Archives, Talladega College, Talladega, Alabama; all other images from the author's collection.

FURTHER READING

BICKFORD, CHRISTOPHER P. *Farmington in Connecticut.* Canaan, N.H.: Phoenix Publishing, 1982.

FILLER, LOUIS. *Crusade Against Slavery.* Algonac, Mich.: Reference Publications, Inc., 1986.

JONES, HOWARD. *Mutiny on the Amistad.* New York: Oxford University Press, 1987.

PETERSON, JOHN. *Province of Freedom: A History of Sierra Leone.* Evanston, Ill.: Northwestern University Press, 1969.

BIBLIOGRAPHY

Books

BROOKE, HENRY K. *Book of Pirates*. Philadelphia: J.B. Perry, 1841.

COMMAGER, HENRY STEELE. *Documents of American History*. New York: Appleton-Century-Crofts, 1958.

Correspondence with the British Commissioners Relating to the Slave Trade for 1845. London: Her Majesty's Stationery Office.

FINKELMAN, PAUL, ED. *The African Slave Trade and American Courts*. New York: Garland, 1988.

INNES, GORDON. *A Mende-English Dictionary*. London: Cambridge University Press, 1969.

LAWSON, ELLEN NICKENZIE, with MARLENE D. MERRILL. *The Three Sarahs: Documents of Ante-bellum Black College Women*. New York: Edwin Mellen Press, 1984.

MAYER, BRANTZ. *Captain Canot, or Twenty Years of an African Slaver*. New York: Appleton, 1866.

THOMPSON, GEORGE. *Thompson in Africa*. Cleveland: D.M. Ide, 1852.

Periodicals

The African Repository, vol. XIV. Washington, D.C.: James C. Dunn, 1838.

Hartford Courant, various contemporary.

London Illustrated News, April 14, 1849.

National Intelligencer, various contemporary.

Niles National Register, various contemporary.

Additional Sources

Farmington Public Library, Farmington, Conn.

Methodist Archives, Drew University, Madison, N.J.

Schomburg Center for Research in Black Culture, New York, N.Y.

INDEX

About the Author

Walter Dean Myers is an acclaimed author of fiction, nonfiction, and poetry for young readers. He has long been fascinated by the Amistad rebellion and by the captives themselves, for he believes that it was in the captives that America first saw the greatness of Africa's people.

Myers has received two Newbery Honors. He is a five-time recipient of the Coretta Scott King Award. He is also a winner of the 1994 SLJ/YALSA Margaret A. Edwards Award for Outstanding Literature for Young Adults and the 1994 ALAN Award.